TOP 10 AMERICAN WOMEN'S FIGURE SKATERS

Margaret Poynter

SPORTS
TOP 10

Enslow Publishers, Inc.

44 Fadem Road   PO Box 38
Box 699   Aldershot
Springfield, NJ 07081 Hants GU12 6BP
USA   UK

Library of Congress Cataloging-in-Publication Data

Poynter, Margaret.
    Top 10 American women's figure skaters / Margaret Poynter.
        p. cm. — (Sports top 10)
    Includes bibliographical references (p. 46) and index.
    Summary: Profiles ten notable women figure skaters in American history,
including Peggy Fleming, Dorothy Hamill, and Kristi Yamaguchi.
    ISBN 0-7660-1075-9
    1. Women skaters—United States—Biography—Juvenile literature.
2. Women skaters—Rating of—United States—Juvenile literature. [1. Women
skaters. 2. Ice skaters. 3. Women—Biography.] I. Title. II. Title: Top 10
American women's figure skaters. III. Series.
GV850.A2P69 1998
796.912'092'273
[B]—dc21   97-27217
                                          CIP
                                       AC r98

Printed in the United States of America

10 9 8 7 6 5 4 3 2 1

Illustration Credits: Courtesy of AP/Wide World Photos, pp. 14, 17;
Courtesy of Mentor Marketing and Management, pp. 39, 41; Courtesy of
Paul and Michelle Harvath, pp. 19, 21, 26, 29, 35, 37, 42, 45; Courtesy of
Proper Marketing Associates, pp. 31, 33; Courtesy of the World Figure
Skating Museum, pp. 6, 9, 11, 13, 22, 25.

Cover Illustration: Courtesy of Paul and Michelle Harvath.

Interior Design: Richard Stalzer

CONTENTS

INTRODUCTION

WHAT DOES IT TAKE TO BECOME a champion figure skater? For starters, it takes time. A champion practices for three to six hours every day. There is little time for television or parties or hanging out with friends.

A champion must have the strength of a gymnast and the grace of a ballet dancer. Her feet may be blistered and her muscles may ache, but each move must appear effortless.

A champion skater must have nerves of steel. During a competition, there is no chance to correct mistakes. If she falls, she must go on with her program as if nothing has happened.

A champion skater must have drive, determination, and discipline. She must learn from each failure and build on each success.

Every American Olympic skater starts her career by joining the United States Figure Skating Association. To participate in the USFSA competitions, she must pass a series of eight tests. The first three tests are preliminary. After passing the fourth test, she ranks as a juvenile. She then advances to the intermediate, novice, junior, and finally senior levels. In the competitions, skaters are classified by skill, not age. Juveniles compete only against other skaters of the same skill level, no matter how old they are.

Competitive skaters begin by entering competitions near their hometown. Local winners move up to one of nine regional competitions. Regional winners go to one of three sectional competitions. Winners in the sectionals advance to the Nationals. Nationals winners then go on to an international competition, such as the World Championships or the Olympics.

An American woman first won an Olympic medal in figure skating in 1956. Since then, in eleven Olympic games, a total of nine gold and silver Olympic medals have been taken by American women. Each of these skaters had her own special problems to overcome before enjoying a successful career.

That is not to say that there have not been other great American women figure skaters. Some Olympic medal winners had to be left out. These include Theresa Weld, Beatrix Loughran, Maribel Vinson, Barbara Roles, Janet Lynn, and Rosalyn Sumners. Each skater that we did choose has proved that she belongs on the list of the greatest American women figure skaters of all time. Here is *our* list.

CAREER STATISTICS

SKATER	NATIONALS	WORLDS	OLYMPICS
TENLEY ALBRIGHT	gold 1952–56	gold 1953, 1955 silver 1954	gold 1956 silver 1952
PEGGY FLEMING	gold 1964–68	gold 1966–68	gold 1968
LINDA FRATIANNE	gold 1977	gold 1977, 79	silver 1980
DOROTHY HAMILL	gold 1974–76	gold 1976 silver 1974, 1975	gold 1976
CAROL HEISS	gold 1957–60 silver 1953, 1954	gold 1956–60 silver 1954	gold 1960 silver 1956
NANCY KERRIGAN	gold 1993 bronze 1991	silver 1992 bronze 1991	silver 1994 bronze 1992
MICHELLE KWAN	gold 1996, 1998 silver 1994, 1995, 1997	gold 1996, 1998 silver 1997	silver 1998
TARA LIPINSKI	gold 1997 silver 1996, 1998	gold 1997	gold 1998
DEBI THOMAS	gold 1986, 88 silver 1985, 1987	gold 1986	bronze 1988
KRISTI YAMAGUCHI	gold 1992 silver 1989–91 *gold 1989, 1990	gold 1991, 1992	gold, 1992

* Indicates performance in pairs competitions.

TENLEY ALBRIGHT

Tenley Albright recovered from polio to achieve her dream of becoming a champion figure skater. The polio virus attacks the nerve cells and can sometimes cause paralysis.

TENLEY ALBRIGHT

TENLEY ALBRIGHT WAS EIGHT YEARS OLD when she decided upon one of her two life goals. First, she wanted to become a champion ice-skater. For a while, her parents did not think she was serious. She was ten before she had her first skating lesson.

Albright didn't get much support at school, either. Her principal objected when she left class early to enter a skating event. By this time, Albright's parents knew she was serious about skating. They sent her to a school with a more understanding principal.

When Tenley Albright was eleven, she was ready to start competing. But then she became ill with polio, a crippling disease. Her case was mild, but it left her with a very weak back. For a while, it seemed as if she would never skate again. But Albright was a fighter. "I was not completely paralyzed, but for a time it was quite scary. I didn't have full use of my leg, neck, and back. Eventually, the doctors allowed me to go back to skating as part of my therapy."[1]

And skate she did. When she was twelve, she won her first competition. A year later, she became national novice champion. Even then, one of her eighth-grade teachers told her to stop wasting her time on skating.

Albright ignored that teacher's advice. In 1952, as a senior, she won the first of her five national championships. Later that year, she won the silver medal in the Olympics. In 1953, Albright became the first American woman figure skater to become world champion.

It was now time for Albright to work on her second goal. She entered college to study to become a doctor. After skating from 4:00 to 6:00 A.M. every day, she went to class, took ballet lessons, and did her homework. She chose to skate at 4:00 A.M., "because that was the only time I could have the rink to myself."[2]

Early in 1954, Albright defended her world championship. During her freestyle program, she fell during a difficult jump. She had to settle for second place. As soon as the competition was over, Albright started practicing the jump she had missed. A year later, she regained her lost title. Before then, no other skater had ever recaptured a world title.

Now, her friends thought, Albright would give up skating and focus on her study of medicine. But the 1956 Olympics were coming up. Albright wanted to win the gold medal to make her skating career complete. "This was the big one she had never won, and she was ready."[3]

Several days before the Olympic figure skating competition, Albright cut herself with her skate. Despite the pain, she performed a daring freestyle program and spun to a breathtaking finish. Tenley Albright was the first American woman to win an Olympic figure skating gold medal.

Tenley Albright had reached one of her goals. A few years later, she reached the second when she became a surgeon. To top off her skating career, in 1983, she was inducted into the International Women's Sports Hall of Fame.

TENLEY ALBRIGHT

BORN: July 18, 1935, Newton Center, Massachusetts.

COLLEGE: Radcliffe College, Cambridge, Massachusetts.

RECORDS/AWARDS: U.S. National Champion, 1952–1956; World Champion, 1953, 1955; Placed second at World Championships, 1954; Won silver medal at the 1952 Winter Olympics; Won gold medal at the 1956 Winter Olympics; Inducted into the International Women's Sports Hall of Fame, 1983; Inducted into U.S. Olympic Hall of Fame, 1988.

At the 1956 Winter Olympics, Tenley Albright became the first American woman to win an Olympic gold medal. The games were held in Cortina d'Ampezzo, Italy.

PEGGY FLEMING

LITTLE PEGGY FLEMING PLAYED every sport the other neighborhood children played. Her knees and elbows were always bruised and skinned. Her mother thought that ice-skating might be a sport Fleming could enjoy without getting hurt.

Mrs. Fleming was right. The first time Peggy skated, she was on the ice for an hour and did not fall. After taking a few lessons, she easily passed the first of eight USFSA tests.

Peggy Fleming had been skating for only a year when she won a skating competition. Winning was easy, she thought. When she was ten, she entered a regional competition. She came in last.

She was confused. How could she be first in one competition and last in another? Then she understood. The first time she had practiced hard and skated her best. The second time she had been too confident. She promised herself that she would never again do less than her best. Fleming had learned an important lesson. She won her next several competitions. In 1962, she came in second as a novice in the Nationals.

The following year, though, she slipped to third place in the Junior Nationals. She admitted that she hadn't skated as well as she could. At fourteen, had she tried to move up too fast? Her determination won over her doubts. In 1964, as a senior skater, she won the first of her five National Championships. Then, she went on to place sixth in the Olympics.

Two years later, Fleming entered the Worlds. She was far ahead of the defending champion, but she didn't let up.

Peggy Fleming was a natural on the ice. She won the very first competition that she entered.

The audience applauded wildly at her graceful moves. Even before her program ended, Fleming knew she had won the world championship. The next year, she followed it up with another gold medal at the Worlds. Now it was time to prepare for the Olympics.

Six years earlier, many of the best American skaters had been killed in a plane crash. Since then, the United States had been trying to rebuild its Olympic skating team. By 1968, its hopes for a gold medal in figure skating fell upon Fleming. She felt the pressure of those hopes.

"Everyone expects me to be perfect," she said. "Living up to everyone's expectations is harder than all the practice hours and training combined."[1]

Fleming handled the stress by thinking of the Olympics as just another competition. "I'll do the best that I can," she said.[2] Again, she was far ahead of her competitors. She could have won by doing an easy routine. Instead, she chose her most difficult jumps, leaps, and spins.

"She floats across the ice like a prima ballerina," said one observer. "She's pure dance."[3]

Fleming won the gold with the highest scores in Olympic history up to that time. A month later, she added her third World Championship. In 1975, Peggy Fleming became the youngest person ever to be inducted into the Skating Hall of Fame. In 1981, she also became a member of the International Women's Sports Hall of Fame.

Fleming's victories were the result of determination and a positive attitude. In 1998, those same traits helped her again when she was stricken with breast cancer. Thirty years to the day she had won Olympic gold, she underwent surgery. The surgery was successful—Fleming would be fine.

Fleming's friends were relieved when they heard the good news. Tara Lipinski spoke for all of them when she said, "Something like this puts skating in perspective."[4]

BORN: July 27, 1948, San Jose, California.

RECORDS/AWARDS: U.S. National Champion, 1964–1968; World Champion, 1966–1968; Won gold medal at 1968 Winter Olympics; Associated Press Female Athlete of the Year, 1968; Inducted into the Skating Hall of Fame, 1975; Inducted into U.S. Olympic Hall of Fame, 1983; Inducted into International Women's Sports Hall of Fame, 1981.

The 1968 U.S. Olympic figure skating team was depending on Peggy Fleming to win a medal. She lived up to their expectations and won the gold.

LINDA FRATIANNE

Linda Fratianne became a world-class skater by practicing her routines for hours and hours.

LINDA FRATIANNE

BEFORE LINDA FRATIANNE ENTERED an ice-skating competition, she pinned a tiny blue pouch to her dress. Inside that pouch were five good-luck charms: two four-leaf clovers, a piece of gold foil, a snip of green yarn, and a medal blessed by the Pope.

Fratianne had a great deal of skating talent, but she depended on neither charms nor talent. She knew that winning is the result of hundreds of hours of practice. Again and again, she did the same spins, loops, and dance steps. She didn't stop until she could do each one perfectly.

"I never stop trying," she said. "No matter how good anyone becomes in anything, there's always something that can be improved."[1]

Linda Fratianne seemed to have been born to skate. By the time she was nine, she had already worn out several pairs of roller skates. That Christmas, she received her first pair of ice skates. Before long, she was entering local competitions. When she was twelve, she took second place in the junior division of the Nationals.

In 1974, when Fratianne was fourteen, she entered the Nationals as a senior. Her program included two triple jumps. No woman in any major competition had ever attempted a triple. Despite her impressive feat, she finished only seventh.

In 1976, fifteen-year-old Fratianne placed second at the Worlds. She then went to the Olympics, where she finished eighth. The following year, she won the National Senior Ladies' title with a nearly flawless performance.

She then went to the 1977 World Championships. To

her, the idea of winning the Worlds seemed like a dream. Then the dream started to fade. On the morning of her freestyle performance, she woke up with an inner ear infection. Her balance was affected. She could barely walk. Maybe I should just give up? she thought.

But Fratianne did not give up. She skated her best program and took the gold medal. After her victory, she went to bed for six days.

Fratianne wanted to get back into training, but her ear problem returned. Then she got a bad ankle sprain. For five weeks, her foot was in a cast. Not being able to skate "drove me crazy," she said.[2]

In 1978, Linda lost the World title, but she was not discouraged. She came back strong the following year and regained the World title. Dick Button, a former Olympic skating champion, likened her performance to that of a firecracker: quick, precise, and energetic.

After every victory and every setback, Linda Fratianne looked toward the 1980 Olympics. There, she won the silver, not the gold. Knowing she had skated her best, she smiled. "There's more to life than winning a gold medal," she said.[3]

LINDA FRATIANNE

BORN: August 2, 1960, Northridge, California.

RECORDS/AWARDS: U.S. National Champion, 1977; World Champion
1977, 1979; Won silver medal at 1980 Winter Olympics;
Named U.S. Olympic Committee Sportswoman of the
Year, 1977.

Despite an inner ear infection, Linda Fratianne won the gold
medal at the 1977 World Championships.

DOROTHY HAMILL

DOROTHY HAMILL LIKED CHALLENGES. When she was eight, ice-skating became her main challenge. By the time she was ten, she had passed all of the USFSA tests and entered her first competition. She liked the excitement of competition. "I feel good," she said about competing. "I feel alive. I feel happy."[1]

At age twelve, Hamill became the National Ladies' Novice Champion. She went on to the Junior Regionals, where she practiced in an empty, poorly lit rink. One morning, she skated full-speed into a rope stretched across the ice. She fell and suffered a concussion, which is a type of head injury. A doctor said she could not skate that night.

Hamill was bitterly disappointed. If she could not finish the regionals, she would miss the sectionals and the nationals. To her delight, the judges decided she could go to the sectionals after all. There, she became the Ladies' Junior Champion for the eastern United States.

In the 1970 Junior Nationals, Dorothy Hamill astounded everyone by adding a sit-spin to another movement, the flying camel. The new move was named the Hamill Camel. At age thirteen, Hamill had won second place. She had also had a figure skating movement named after her.

Hamill won the silver in the 1973 Nationals. In the next Nationals, she was prepared and eager. During her jumps, she appeared to drift up and hang in midair. Her landings ended in dizzying spins. She was athletic, but graceful. Her jumps were sensational. At the young age of seventeen, she had become the national champion.

Hamill then flew to West Germany for the 1974 World

In the 1970 Junior Nationals, Dorothy Hamill created a new skating movement, the Hamill Camel.

DOROTHY HAMILL

Championships. She received high marks on her short (technical) program. She was only a little nervous as she glided onto the ice for her long (freestyle) program. Then the crowd began to boo. Confused, Hamill left the ice. She was told that the booing was for the judges. They had given low marks to the hometown favorite, who had just finished skating.

Hamill returned to the ice, but the booing continued. She burst into tears. Trembling, she left the ice again. The officials asked her if she wanted to rest. She took a deep breath. "I'm ready to skate," she said.[2] After her program, she received a roaring ovation. The silver medal was hers.

Two months before the 1975 Nationals, Hamill injured her foot and could not practice, but she skated well enough to retain her title. With her foot still hurting, she then won the silver at the 1976 Worlds. She also won the gold medal at the Nationals for the third time.

At the 1976 Olympics, Hamill's short program put her far ahead of her competitors. She could have won with an easy freestyle routine. Instead, she challenged herself with her most difficult leaps and spins. She won the Olympic gold, then went on to win the world championship.

Dorothy Hamill had become only the fourth American woman to win all of the national and international figure skating titles.

DOROTHY HAMILL

BORN: July 26, 1956, Chicago, Illinois.

HIGH SCHOOL: Greenwich High School, Greenwich, Connecticut.

RECORDS/AWARDS: U.S. National Champion, 1974–1976; World Champion, 1976; Placed second at World Championships, 1974–1975; Won gold medal at 1976 Winter Olympics; Inducted into the U.S. Olympic Hall of Fame, 1991; Inducted into U.S. Figure Skating Hall of Fame, 1991.

Dorothy Hamill won both the Olympic gold medal and the World Championships in 1976.

CAROL HEISS

After winning the 1960 Olympic gold medal, Carol Heiss dedicated the award to her mother, who had passed away a few years before the Olympic Games.

CAROL HEISS WAS ALMOST FIVE when she started to ice-skate. From her first time on the ice, Heiss showed a perfect sense of balance. Her teacher urged Heiss's parents to hire a special skating instructor. Such lessons are very expensive. Mr. Heiss made just enough money to support his family. He asked the teacher how far Carol could go if she were given skating lessons.

The teacher said, "We believe that if she studies hard, in ten years she can be champion of the world."[1] Mrs. Heiss immediately took a part-time job to make extra money.

The lessons and rink fees were not the only expenses. Carol needed piano lessons to improve her sense of rhythm. She needed ballet lessons to develop her style. Carol's parents worked longer hours. Carol wore homemade skating costumes.

Carol seemed to be fulfilling her skating teacher's prediction. She was only ten when she won her first two titles, the Middle Atlantic Regionals and the National Juniors.

Now there were more expenses: better skates and fares to competitions. At age thirteen, Heiss went to Switzerland for the World Championships, where she placed fourth. A few months later, she placed second in the 1953 North American competition and the Senior Nationals.

Carol's career had a setback when she was skating with her sister, Nancy. During a collision, Nancy's skate slashed Carol's foot. Carol couldn't practice for several months. Meanwhile, Mrs. Heiss had become very ill with cancer.

Carol wanted to become a gold medalist before her mother died. But in the 1954 National and North American

Championships, she again took second place. At the Worlds, she also won the silver.

Heiss then started practicing for the 1956 Olympics. At sixteen, she became the youngest female ever to skate on the United States team. Her performance was called the most daring ever presented by a female Olympic skater. Again, though, she missed out on the gold medal. Instead, she took the silver.

By then, Mrs. Heiss's health was failing fast. All of Carol's energy went into preparing for the upcoming Worlds. All of her skill and artistry went into her performance. Mrs. Heiss was able to see her daughter win the first of her five world championships. She died soon afterward. In 1957, Carol won the first of her four national championships.

At the 1960 Olympics, Heiss became America's second figure skating gold medalist. As the ribbon was placed around her neck, she whispered, "It's for you, Mother. I promised."[2]

In 1992, Carol Heiss was inducted into the International Women's Sports Hall of Fame.

BORN: January 20, 1940, Ozone Park, New York.

RECORDS/AWARDS: U. S. National Champion, 1957–1960; Placed second at National Championships, 1953–1954; World Champion, 1956–1960; Placed second at World Championships, 1954; Won silver medal at 1956 Winter Olympics; Won gold medal at 1960 Winter Olympics; Inducted into the International Women's Sports Hall of Fame, 1992.

Carol Heiss has been a member of the International Women's Sports Hall of Fame since 1992.

NANCY KERRIGAN

Nancy Kerrigan had to overcome her own negative thoughts to compete in national and international competitions. By believing in herself, she was able to accomplish all her dreams in skating.

IT WAS SIX-YEAR-OLD NANCY KERRIGAN'S first skating class, but Kerrigan didn't wait for the teacher to appear. She went onto the ice and did some spins. She felt she could do jumps before she tried them.

Nancy Kerrigan was almost right. As a "natural skater," she froze the image of a jump into her mind. Then all she had to do was to practice it again and again. She became the first woman to master triple-jump combinations.

Kerrigan was nine when she started competing. For a while, she always placed first or second. Those wins caused her to worry about what people would think if she performed poorly. She became very nervous. In 1985, she placed ninth as a novice in her first Nationals. In her next Nationals, she placed eleventh.

She now knew that nervousness was not her only problem. The image of a total jump didn't allow her to see the jump's separate parts. Judges noticed those small parts. Kerrigan had to correct some bad habits.

Her work paid off in the 1987 Junior Nationals, where she placed fourth. The following year, though, she dropped to eleventh place as a senior in the Nationals. But in the same year, she won two international competitions. The next January, she was fifth in the Nationals.

Competitions still made Kerrigan very nervous. At the 1990 Nationals, a voice inside her head whispered, "You can't do this."[1] She came in fourth, so she couldn't go to the Worlds. The next year, in the same competition, she fell. Then, during a triple, she did only two spins. If she made one more mistake, she wouldn't qualify to go to the Worlds again.

Kerrigan forced herself to ignore the voice. She won the bronze medal and went to her first Worlds, where she took the bronze. One year later, she took third place in the 1992 Olympics. The next month, she placed second at the Worlds. In 1993, she took first place in the Nationals.

At the next Worlds, though, the voice came back. "You can't do this," it said.[2] Kerrigan was so nervous, her body felt stiff. Three triple jumps became singles or doubles. She took fifth place. To Kerrigan, her performance had seemed like a bad dream.

The next year, 1994, was an Olympic year. If Kerrigan were to go to the Games, she had to do well in the Nationals. Every day, she practiced her entire program over and over again. She was preparing herself to win.

One day, she had just finished a long practice. As she walked to her dressing room, she sensed that someone was behind her. When she turned around, she saw a man raise his arm, then bring it downward. In his hand was a metal rod, which struck her knee. The pain was intense. Kerrigan fell to the floor, screaming.

It was later found out that the attack had been planned by some associates of Kerrigan's chief competitor, Tonya Harding. They had hoped to keep Kerrigan out of the Nationals. Sure enough, Kerrigan was hurt too badly to compete. However, the United States Olympic Committee added Kerrigan to the team. Kerrigan had to endure painful therapy, but she was able to compete in the Olympics.

At the Games, Nancy Kerrigan doubled her first triple jump. She went on to give the finest performance of her life. She won the silver, losing the gold by only a tenth of a point to Ukranian skater Oksana Baiul.

"I believed in myself," she said. "Now the voice tells me that anything is possible."[3]

NANCY KERRIGAN

BORN: October 13, 1969, Woburn, Massachusetts.

COLLEGE: Emmanuel College, Boston, Massachusetts.

RECORDS/AWARDS: U.S. National Champion, 1993; Placed second at
World Championships, 1992; Placed third at World
Championships, 1991; Won bronze medal at 1992 Winter
Olympics; Won silver medal at 1994 Winter Olympics.

Nancy Kerrigan had to endure months of rehabilitation from a
knee injury to make the 1994 Olympic team. She not only
recovered in time, but did well enough to win a silver medal.

MICHELLE KWAN

IS IT POSSIBLE to be a perfect ice-skater? Maybe not, but Michelle Kwan wanted to come as close to perfection as she could. She started to skate when she was five. A year later, she won her first competition. At the 1992 Junior Nationals, she finished sixth. The low rating made her work harder than ever.

"I wanted to challenge myself against the best," she said.[1]

Her coach prepared Kwan for future challenges. One morning, she arrived at practice feeling sick, but her coach coaxed her to skate. "Imagine you have the flu, you feel dizzy and terrible, but it's the Olympics," he said. Kwan went on to have a long practice session. She did the same jumps again and again until her body was like a programmed machine. Her routine was the toughest ever performed by a woman. It had eight jumps, seven of them triples. Three jumps occurred in the final minute, when skaters are very tired.

In 1993, as a senior at the Nationals, Kwan again placed sixth. The next year, she came in second, and in 1995, took second place in the Nationals and fourth in the Worlds. In 1996, when she was fifteen, she became the youngest national champion in over thirty years.

Later that year, going into her freestyle at the Worlds, Michelle Kwan trailed China's Lu Chen. Kwan grew nervous as she heard Lu Chen's high scores. "Those are fabulous marks," said her coach, "but they left you room to win."[2]

Kwan's confidence returned. She became the youngest American ever to win the Worlds.

MICHELLE KWAN

In 1998, Michelle Kwan won both the U.S. Nationals and the World Championships.

By 1997, Michelle Kwan had won six consecutive competitions. By February, she was a favorite to win the Nationals. But the pressure of defending her title was hard to handle. Her first jump was good, but at the end of a jump combination, she tumbled onto the ice. After falling out of the next triple loop, she managed to keep from going all the way down. On the next triple loop, though, she went crashing to the ice.

Because of her good scores in the short program, Kwan placed second in the competition. It was a disappointing moment for her. But after drying her tears, she said, "I have to learn something from this. You have to learn how to take defeat. I've been skating more not to lose than to win. I've got to start going for it again.

"I've taken a fall," she continued, "but I'll stand up and fight again."[3]

She was true to her word. At the 1997 Worlds, she performed an almost perfect freestyle program and won the silver medal.

"I've learned the lesson that everyone works hard, everyone wants it, and in the end, the strongest will win," she said.[4]

And Michelle Kwan is strong. According to her coach, "She looks like a little flower, but inside there's a core of metal, a strength that's unbelievable."[5]

That strength was with her as she glided onto the ice during the 1998 Olympics. Despite an excellent performance, she came in second. After shedding a few tears, Kwan dried her eyes. "I came here to do a job," she said. "I worked very hard. I skated well."[6]

Later, when asked how she felt about losing the gold medal, Kwan smiled. "I didn't lose the gold. I won the silver."[7] She was already thinking, "What can I do better in the next Olympics?"[8]

MICHELLE KWAN

BORN: July 7, 1980, Torrance, California.

RECORDS/AWARDS: U.S. National Champion, 1996, 1998; Placed
second at U.S. National Championships, 1994–1995, 1997;
World Champion, 1996, 1998; Placed second at World
Championships, 1997; Won silver medal at 1998 Olympics.

Michelle Kwan, along with Tara Lipinski and Nicole Bobek,
represented the United States at the Olympics in Nagano, Japan.

TARA LIPINSKI

TARA LIPINSKI LEARNED HOW TO ROLLER-SKATE when she was three. She was five when she started playing roller hockey with boys who were older than she was. At the same age, she won her first roller-skating competition. From the beginning, Lipinski liked competition of any sort.

When she was six, Lipinski learned to ice-skate because "she had nothing better to do."[1] Five years later, she won the Nationals as a novice. In 1995, at the age of twelve, she took the silver as a junior at the Nationals and placed fourth in the Worlds junior event.

In these events, Lipinski was always the youngest person competing. At this time of her life, her goal was simple. "I just want to do my best," she said. "I try to skate cleanly and leave the rest up to the judges."[2]

In 1996, Lipinski came in third as a senior at the Nationals. She was now qualified to compete as a senior in the upcoming Worlds. She didn't win a medal, but she was not discouraged. To prepare for the next competition, she continued to spend four hours a day on the ice. She also went to ballet and aerobics classes and did four hours of schoolwork.

As the 1997 Nationals drew near, she felt ready, but she did not think she would win the gold. "I just wanted to skate two great programs," she said. "My goal was to make the world team."[3]

Tara Lipinski did skate two great programs. She performed seven clean triple jumps and became the youngest United States champion in history. Her program contained a triple-jump combination that had never before been seen

TARA LIPINSKI

In 1997, at the age of fourteen, Tara Lipinski became the youngest national champion ever. Then, later in the same year, she won the gold at the Worlds, and became the youngest world champion in history.

in a national championship. One reporter described Lipinski as "a jumping dynamo."[4]

"Technically, the program Tara did will give any woman in the world a run for the money," said her coach.[5]

At the beginning of the 1997 competitive season, Lipinski traveled from the United States to Canada to France to Germany. Again and again, she competed with the world's best skaters. "It was a bit overwhelming," she said, "but once I was on the ice, I knew I was prepared. I love the thrill of competing."[6]

As a fourteen-year-old going into the Worlds, Lipinski was bound to feel pressure. But she was not worried. "Last year, I finished fifteenth, so I figure I can only get better. I'm still not expecting to win or place. I just want it to be my best."[7]

Lipinski chose a long program that would have been difficult for someone with twice her experience. But Lipinski was cool under pressure. Her fierce determination carried her through perfect jump after perfect jump. Her difficult, breathtaking performance won her the gold medal. She was the youngest U.S. figure skater ever to win the world championships.

Tara Lipinski's goal had progressed to "be the best in the world at what I do."[8] In February 1998 she reached that goal. At the age of fifteen, she became the youngest Olympic figure skating gold medalist in history. She squealed and jumped up and down when she saw her winning scores.

"I can't believe it!" she cried. "There is nothing that could be better than this night!"[9]

TARA LIPINSKI

BORN: June 10, 1982, Philadelphia, Pennsylvania.

RECORDS/AWARDS: U.S. National Champion, 1997; Placed second at
U.S. National Championships, 1996; World Champion,
1997; Youngest woman to ever win a world figure skating
championship; 1997 U.S. Olympic Committee
Sportswoman of the Year; Olympic Gold Medalist, 1998;
Youngest woman to ever win an Olympic figure skating
gold medal.

Michelle Kwan and Tara Lipinski competed against each other in
the Nationals and again in the Olympics in 1998. Despite finishing
behind Kwan at the U.S. Nationals, Lipinski won the gold medal at
the Games in Nagano.

DEBI THOMAS

"WHY DO THEY THROW FLOWERS? Why not pizza?"[1] "I want to be the first skater in space. Once you start spinning, you'd never stop."[2]

Debi Thomas had a sense of humor about her skating. That attitude helped her when things didn't go right.

More important than her sense of humor was the way she thought about herself. "I'm invincible," she once wrote. "Its hard to tell what keeps me going. I guess it's a dream that has to be finished."[3]

Thomas's dream began when she was five and went to an ice show. Her mother had only enough money for used skates. The boots were too small. When the skates were broken, Debi fixed them with glue. She was ten before she got a coach. She soon began to sew her own skating costumes.

Thomas practiced six hours a day and still did well in school. Her grades were important because she wanted to become a doctor.

In 1985, Debi placed second in the Nationals. When she entered Stanford University, she became the first woman in thirty years to compete while attending college. During her first year, she was overwhelmed with schoolwork. She tore up the 1986 Nationals entry form, but kept the pieces. After a short vacation, she taped the form together, entered the competition, and won first place. She went on to win the gold at the Worlds.

By 1987, Thomas was "drowning in schoolwork." She also had two throbbing Achilles tendons. Nevertheless, she entered both the Worlds and the Nationals. She was unable

DEBI THOMAS

After tearing up her entry form for the 1986 Nationals, Debi Thomas decided to give the competition a shot. She won the gold at that competition, and then won the Worlds in the same year.

to defend either of her championships, but she did finish second at the Nationals.

Thomas refused to give up her dream. She liked the feeling she had when she was competing. "You're so high," she said. "A tingle goes through your whole body. If you've done something and you know it's right, it's like 'Ahhh.' The people can see it in your face, and it reflects off them right back to you."[4]

In 1988, Thomas regained her Nationals title. "If you trust your nerve as well as your skill," she said, "you're capable of a lot more than you can imagine."[5]

Now the Olympics were coming up. Thomas took fewer courses at Stanford, so she could practice more. As she skated, she talked to herself. "I'm going to eat this one alive . . . I conquered that jump . . . extra energy now . . . here it comes!"[6]

Thomas became the first African-American member of the U.S. Olympic skating team. The United States hadn't had a female figure skating gold medalist in twelve years. Thomas was the best hope for a ladies' gold medal, but she won the bronze instead.

"I never wanted to feel that if I didn't win the gold medal, I was nothing," she said. "Things like the importance of an education and being whatever you can be give me the inner strength to pull things off on the ice."[7]

That inner strength also enabled Debi Thomas to become a medical doctor. She obtained her degree in June 1997. As a doctor and a champion skater, she hopes "to help people learn to live together in harmony and respect each other's differences."[8]

DEBI THOMAS

BORN: March 25, 1967, Poughkeepsie, N.Y.

HIGH SCHOOL: San Mateo High School, San Mateo, California.

COLLEGE: Stanford University, Northwestern University.

RECORDS/AWARDS: U.S. National Champion, 1986, 1988; Placed
second at U.S. National Championships, 1985, 1987;
World Champion, 1986; Won bronze medal at
1988 Winter Olympics.

Debi Thomas was not only a great skater, but also a fantastic
student. She became a doctor after her figure skating career ended.

KRISTI YAMAGUCHI

Kristi Yamaguchi excelled in both singles and pairs skating. At the 1989 Nationals, she won two medals: a gold in pairs competition and a silver in singles.

KRISTI YAMAGUCHI

IT WAS A TURNED-IN FOOT CONDITION that started Kristi Yamaguchi's journey to the Olympics. When she was four years old, her parents signed her up for ballet lessons. Two years later, she started ice-skating lessons. Her doctors hoped that dance and skating would correct her foot problem.

Little Kristi Yamaguchi was not very strong, but she was determined to pass the USFSA tests. She exercised. She practiced skating every day. She took dancing lessons.

In 1986, Yamaguchi became the Central Pacific junior champion. She then came in fourth as a junior in the Nationals. Two years later, in the World Junior competition, she won the gold with her singles performance. She and her skating partner, Rudy Galindo, also won first place in the pairs event.

At the 1989 Nationals, Yamaguchi took a gold in pairs and a silver in singles. She was the first woman in thirty-five years to win two medals at the same Nationals. Then, at the Worlds, she finished sixth in singles and fifth in pairs. Despite those scores, many people were sure she would go to the Olympics. But Yamaguchi was not sure. "The Olympics are three years away," she said. "Anything could happen."[1]

At the 1990 Nationals, Yamaguchi won the silver as a single, and she and Galindo won another pairs title. But in the World's pairs, they came in fifth. Yamaguchi decided to focus on her career as a single. It was not an easy decision. "I miss pairs terribly," she said. "There is something about working with someone out there on the ice and having the same goals together."[2]

It seemed as if Kristi Yamaguchi had made the right choice. She finished out the year by winning three important competitions. Then, in 1991, she took the gold medal at the Worlds.

At this time, some experts believed that Yamaguchi would not do well in the upcoming Olympics. She was an artistic skater. Her routine was built around graceful dance steps. Her chief rivals were athletic skaters who depended on spectacular jumps.

Yamaguchi herself didn't believe she would win the Olympic gold. During her short program, she skated "as if all that mattered was making people smile," one reporter wrote.[3]

Yamaguchi's long program was almost perfect. It was reported that she was "a feathery vision of artistic precision and elegance."[4] Kristi Yamaguchi won the gold.

As she accepted the medal, she was relieved that the pressure was off. At the same time, she felt a deep sense of loss. "This is the Olympics," she said later. "I had always dreamed of it, always, my whole life. I didn't want it to be over yet."

"The experience of competing in the Games is a greater prize than any medal. I believe there are no Olympic losers."[5]

Later that year, Yamaguchi won her second world championship in a row. She was the first American woman since 1968 to defend that title successfully.

BORN: July 12, 1971, Hayward, California.

RECORDS/AWARDS: U.S. National Champion, 1992; Placed second at U.S. National Championships, 1989–1991; World Champion, 1991–1992; Won gold medal at 1992 Winter Olympics; U.S. National Champion in pairs competition with Rudy Galindo, 1989–1990.

Kristi Yamaguchi did not think she would win an Olympic gold medal. But at the 1992 Winter Olympics in Albertville, France, she won the gold in the women's singles competition.

CHAPTER NOTES

Tenley Albright

1. "Tenley Albright," Bud Greenspan's Olympic Profiles, *Sports Illustrated*, January 12, 1998, special advertising insert between pp. 16–17.

2. "Triumph by Miss Albright Today Would Complete Her Collection," *The New York Times*, February 2, 1956, p. 28.

3. Fred Tupper, "Tenley Albright and Miss Heiss Finish One, Two in Olympic Figure Skating," *The New York Times*, February 3, 1956, p. 26.

Peggy Fleming

1. Elizabeth Van Steenwyck, *Women in Sports* (New York: Harvey House, 1976), p. 31.

2. Ibid.

3. Ibid., p. 40.

4. Karen S. Schneider, "Gold Mettle," *People* Online, March 2, 1998, <http://www.pathfinder.com/people/980302/features/fleming.html> (April 10, 1998).

Linda Fratianne

1. Elizabeth Van Steenwyck, *Stars on Ice* (New York: Dodd, Mead, 1980), p. 25.

2. Ibid., p. 34.

3. Ibid., p. 38.

Dorothy Hamill

1. Edward F. Nolan, Jr., and Richard B. Lytle, *Dorothy Hamill* (New York: Doubleday, 1979), p. 4.

2. Ibid., p. 45.

Carol Heiss

1. Robert Parker, *Carol Heiss: Olympic Queen* (Garden City, N.Y.: Doubleday, 1961), p. 27.

2. Ibid., p. 14.

Nancy Kerrigan

1. Nancy Kerrigan, *In My Own Words* (New York: Hyperion Books for Children, 1996), p. 25.

2. Ibid., pp. 43–44.

3. Ibid., p. 68.

Michelle Kwan

1. Mark Starr, "Iron Will, Golden Dreams," *Newsweek*, February 17, 1997, p. 54.

2. Ibid., p. 53.

3. Ibid.

4. Mark Starr, "Dueling on the Ice," *Newsweek*, March 17, 1997, p. 64.

5. Starr, "Iron Will, Golden Dreams," p. 64.

6. Mike Penner, *Los Angeles Times*, February 21, 1998, p. A14.

7. Appearance on *The Tonight Show*, February 23, 1998.

8. Mark Starr, "Tara's Joy," *Newsweek*, March 2, 1998, p. 64.

Tara Lipinski

1. Press release from Edge Marketing and Management, Charlotte, N.C.

2. Mark Starr, "Dueling on the Ice," *Newsweek*, March 17, 1997, p. 65.

3. Press release from Edge Marketing and Management, Charlotte, N.C., 1997.

4. Ibid.

5. Ibid.

6. Ibid.

7. Ibid.

8. Ibid.

9. Mike Penner, *Los Angeles Times*, February 21, 1998, p. A14.

Debi Thomas

1. Tom Callahan, "The Word She Uses Is 'Invincible,'" *Time*, vol. 131, February 15, 1988, p. 46.

2. Ibid.

3. Ibid.

4. Ibid., p. 48.

5. Ibid.

6. Ibid.

7. Ibid., p. 44.

8. Press release from Mentor Marketing and Management, South Bend, Ind.

Kristi Yamaguchi

1. "A Skating Sprite with a Towering Talent, Kristi Yamaguchi Wants to Ice the World Title," *People Weekly*, vol. 31, March 20, 1989, p. 71.

2. Interview on *ABC Sports*.

3. E. M. Swift, "All That Glitters," *Sports Illustrated*, December 14, 1992, p. 71.

4. Ibid., p. 72.

5. Ibid., p. 75.

INDEX